BRITISH RAIL IN THE EIGHTIES:
LEICESTERSHIRE

PAUL A. BIGGS
BRADGATE PUBLISHING

ACKNOWLEDGMENTS

This book is dedicated to Sandy Copley whose patience and understanding has been endless and without her assistance the book would not have been possible.

Copyright © P A BIGGS 1989
British Rail in the Eighties - Leicestershire.
Pbk. ISBN 0 9514590 0 7

Typesetting and Printing by:
Hemmings and Capey Ltd., Ireton Avenue, Leicester
Design: S M Copley
Published by: Bradgate Publishing
15 Mardale Way, Loughborough, Leics.

All photographs are by the author

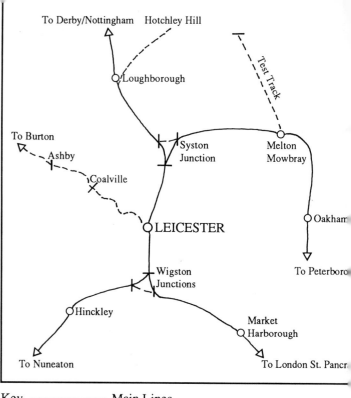

Front cover - 4472 'The Flying Scotsman' brings into Leicester, the empty Pullman stock of Cromwell Tools, Wigston Charter, 'The Cromwell Pullman' to take factory buyers back from South Wigston station to Birmingham New Street on 3 June 1987.

Back cover - Class 45/1 Locomotives No's 45145 and 45110 Double Head the IC28 1658 Sun only Derby-London St Pancras service on 16 June 1985 seen powering away from Leicester.

Title - On a very cold 16 January 1985 Class 45/1 No. 45106 is seen at Hinckley, hauling a departmental coach from Willesden Carriage Sidings to Derby Etches Park for repair at Litchurch Lane works.

Right - Three Class 108 two car Tyseley DMU Sets No's 51922 & 54493, 51909 & 54271, and 54257 & 51919 wait at Leicester Station on 24 May 1986 with the 0810 Leicester - Skegness 'Jolly Fisherman' service. Alongside an IC 125 HST waits with the 0740 Nottingham - London St Pancras service

The county of Leicestershire is served by two passenger lines, the Midland Mainline from Sheffield to London St Pancras and the cross country line from Birmingham to Norwich. There is a very strong possibility that a third passenger line will be in existence soon from Leicester to Ashby-de-la-Zouch which currently is freight only and extends to Burton-on-Trent.

During the Eighties many changes and improvements have been made to passenger services, Motive Power, Signalling, Track alterations and the opening of a new station at South Wigston. In the late seventies Leicester Station received substantial investment to modernise the platform buildings and passenger footbridge. This work has continued through the eighties with a new Booking Hall complex opening, containing, Enquiries, Ticket Office, W H Smith and Buffet Take-away facilities. Major construction work continues outside the station on London Road improving road facilities adjoining the Victorian Station.

October 1982 saw the introduction of High Speed Trains (HST) 125 sets ousting Class 45 'Peak' Locomotives on the majority of Midland Mainline services, although it was not until May 1988 that Class 45's became a thing of the past. However, even then one early morning to London and return late evening service remained and this often found Class 45 sole survivor celebrity 45106 at the helm. The major innovation to the Birmingham - Norwich line was the introduction of Class 150/1 Sprinters in May 1986 reducing travelling time and improving passenger comfort. The following year saw the introduction of a new service between Coventry and Nottingham via Leicester and in May 1988 Class 156/4 Super Sprinters took control of Birmingham - Norwich services relieving Class 31/4 locomotives of this task so long associated with this line.

Semaphore signalling became obsolete in 1987 on the Midland Mainline when Phase 2 and Phase 3 of the Leicester Gap multiple aspect colour lights were completed. Phase One of the scheme from Leicester to Glendon Junction was commissioned into service on 29 June 1986, with Phase Two from Leicester to Loughborough starting April 1987 and finally Phase Three between Glendon Junction and Wellingborough opening on 7 December 1987 all controlled from the new Leicester Power Signal Box. Hand in hand with the Leicester Gap m.a.s. major alterations were made to track layouts between Kilby Bridge and Syston Junction with reversible line working very evident in this area.

Freight traffic in Leicestershire is quite substantial with three major quarries at Bardon Hill, Croft and Mountsorrel providing work for the Leicester pool of Class 56 locomotives. The majority of the freight uses the Syston - Melton Mowbray - Manton Junction line including the twice daily 'Tubeliner' from Lackenby to Corby B.S.C. which brings 2 Class 37 locomotives working in tandem to the area. The Birmingham - Peterborough line produces freight running through Leicester Station, which includes cement from Ketton, Stamford, fuel oil from Bedworth and coal to Three Spires, Coventry from Toton Yard.

More recently Leicester has become famous through the activities of Vic Berry, Scrap Merchant, disposing of aging and asbestos condemned locomotives which has resulted in rail enthusiasts affectionately adopting Leicester in the eighties as Barry was in the sixties with the passing of the steam locomotive.
January 1989

Paul A. Biggs
Loughborough

eft upper - Passing the Brush Works at oughborough is Class 31/4 No. 31415 n 16 August 1988 with a Bedford - Jottingham parcels working. Under ectorisation this locomotive has been llocated to the parcels sector and will ot therefore be seen again in charge of assenger services as once was the case.

Left lower - Ready to depart from Loughborough stone sidings on 2 November 1983 is Class 46 No. 46017 in charge of the 6E69 Ballast working to York Leeman Road CCE Sidings. The warehouse seen in the photograph has since been raised to the ground and Loughborough signal box also seen was demolished under phase 2 of the Leicester Gap re-signalling scheme in April 1987.

Above - Celebrity Class 45/1 No. 45106 enters Loughborough Station in murky light on 24 October 1988 with the 0712 Derby-London St Pancras service. This 'Peak' has been specially retained for hauling railtours at weekends and during the week it is normally rostered for this duty and the return evening balanced diagram from London St Pancras.

Left - GWR Brunswick Green Class 47/4 No. 47484 'Isambard Kingdom Brunel' waits at Loughborough Station on 15 May 1988 heading the 1215 Sun only Derby-London St Pancras service. This was the last loco hauled Sunday service as the introduction of the 1988/89 timetable on the following day upgraded this service to HST status.

Right - Thundering down the Midland Mainline at Cossington on 17 August 1985 are Class 20 locomotives no's 20157 and 20121 in charge of the IM02 1205 SO Skegness-Leicester summer only service.

Left- Customised class 45/0 No. 45013 passes Sileby signal box on the slow line on 29 October 1985 powering the 7A84 Toton West Yard-Willesden Brent Sidings ABS Railfreight.

7

Above - Two for the price of one on 25 February 1988. Class 58 No's 58010 and 58006 Double Head the 6E54 Ratcliffe Power Station-Fletton Flyash empties seen on the slow line at Cossington approaching Syston North Junction. 58006 had failed earlier and 58010 was sent from Toton to haul forward the train to avoid risking a financial penalty through late arrival.

Right upper - During August 1983 Class 58 No. 58001 was seen most days undergoing tests to eradicate teething troubles with this new class. On 25 August 1983 the prototype '58' is seen at Cossington with test car 6 and two departmental research units from Derby Works heading towards Leicester.

Right lower - Making an occasional appearance on the Midland Mainline is a Class 40 locomotive No. 40099 seen at Cossington hauling the 7E98 Mountsorrel Sidings - Hitchin CCE ballast working, on 22 November 1983.

Left - At the site of the former Syston Station is Class 31/4 No. 31462 hauling the 1M37 0737 Norwich-Birmingham New Street service on 26 March 1986. In the distance is Syston South Junction where the Peterborough line joins the Midland line for traffic heading to and from Leicester. On the extreme right is Blue Circle's cement depot and sidings.

Right - Slowly joining the Midland Mainline at Syston North Junction is Class 31 No. 31317 in Railfreight Livery seen on the slow line on 26 March 1986 with the 7F45 1250SX Bedford South Sidings-Loughborough ballast empties.

Departmental Special Purpose Vehicle Class 97/2 No. 97204 waits at Syston North
Junction on 13 June 1988 with ADB 975813 a former APT test coach converted in 1979
from HST power car W43000 and two Mk3 coaches separated by brake vans heading for
Old Dalby Test track from Derby Research Centre.

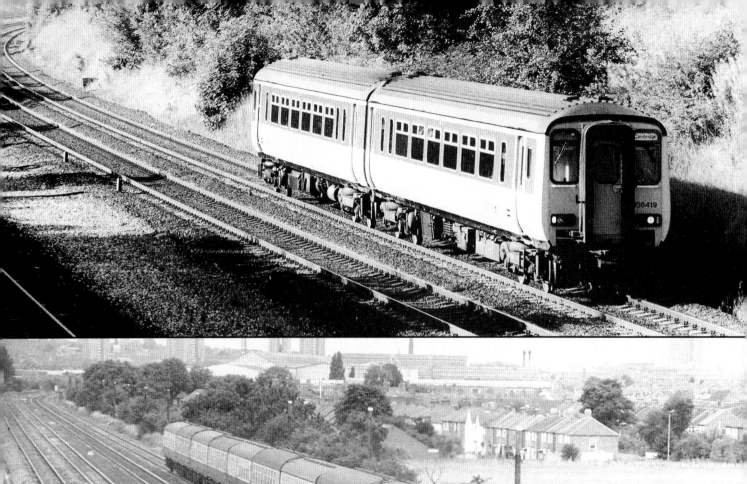

Left upper - Super Sprinter Class 156 No. 156419 is seen in the early morning sunshine at Barkby on 16 August 1988 with the 0741 Birmingham New Street-Cambridge service.

Left lower - At Thurmaston on Sunday 1 September 1985 are 'Choppers' 20163 and 20185 in charge of the 1E26 0823 Leicester-Skegness service. This was the last day of the 1985 'Jolly Fisherman' and for the Class 20's as Class 108 DMU sets were introduced the following year until 1988 when loco hauled stock was re-introduced.

Above - Cromwell Tools, Wigston Pullman Charter 'The Cromwell Pullman' is seen leaving Leicester at Bell Lane on Sunday 7 June 1986 with ScotRail Class 47No. 47461 'Charles Rennie Mackintosh' in charge of the 1L03 to Straford-upon-Avon outward working.

Far left - Class 45/1 No. 45145 pulls away from Leicester Station on 1 April 1986 and is seen passing Leicester North signal box with the 1E89 0848 Leicester-Skegness 'Jolly Fisherman' service. From May 1986 Class 108 DMU sets were noted on this service much to the dismay of haulage enthusiasts.

Left - In appalling weather conditions of freezing driving snow and very little daylight Class 47 No. 47582 'County of Norfolk' passes Leicester North signal box on 5 February 1986 with the 1Z01 Sunderland-Wolverton Works Royal Train E.C.S. The Royal Train had conveyed HRH Prince Charles to Tyneside earlier in the day. Note the second coach having been converted from HST stock and renumbered 2916.

Lower left - Part of the Leicester Gap re-signalling scheme involved substantial track alterations around the station area. On 15 June 1986 the freight lines are being re-aligned alongside Leicester North signal box with RCE heavy duty crane No. 81531 about to swing a new piece of track into place. 45051 heads an engineers spoil train in the Holding Sidings.

Left - A general view of Leicester Locomotive Holding Sidings on 10 January 1986. Once a major depot, but now relegated to a Re-fuelling point it is but a pale shadow of its former self. Seen at the re-fuelling bay is Class 56 No. 56080 and Class 47 No. 47438 with 20010 and 20214 on an adjacent line. Alongside them are 47363 and 47011 with Class 25 No.'s 25313, 25072 and 08465 on the withdrawn line.

Right - Withdrawn Norwich Class 03 No. 03197 was an unusual resident at Leicester Holding Sidings for many months. The diesel shunter is seen minus coupling rods on 29 July 1987 awaiting a decision as to whether the local fitters would be allowed to strip the '03' of its working parts for sale to the preservations societies.

Above - Railfreight liveried Class 31/1 No. 31209 approaches Leicester on the avoiding line on 18 September 1986 with the 6M44 Ward Sidings, Ketton-Castle Bromwich cement train about to pass the derelict Leicester North signal box in the process of being demolished.

Right - Experimental double railbus DMU Class 140 No. 140001 (55500 and 55501) waits at Leicester Station on 23 September 1983 about to depart back to Derby Research Centre on transmission tests.

A scene now of the past but one which typified Leicester Station for more years than one cares to remember. Class 45 'Peak' No. 45141 deputising for a non available HST set waits at the snow covered platform 2 with the 1210 London St Pancras-Nottingham service on 8 January 1986.

Class 37/4 No. 37428 'David Lloyd George' enters Leicester Station on 21 October 1988 with the 1C72 1530 FO Derby-London St Pancras service. In the station sidings is Class 128 DMLV No. 55992 parcels unit in Royal Mail livery. This new Friday Only diagram started on 7 October 1988 bringing a Cardiff based 37/4 from Shrewsbury, collecting the stock off Oxley CS and on to Derby to work the service to London returning at 18.20 to Derby.

Left - Ultrasonic Test Train VUR 505 belonging to Matix Industries and on loan to B.R. Civil Engineers Dept. was an unusual visitor to Leicester Station Holding Sidings on 26 June 1985. Also seen behind is the present Ultrasonic Test Train No.'s DB975008 and DB975007.

Right - In brilliant sunshine Class 31 No. 31327 powers away from Leicester on 9 September 1986 seen at Welford Road in charge of the 6M44 SX Ward Sidings, Ketton-Castle Bromwich Cement Sidings company cement train. This working also carries a penalty for late delivery.

Left - Class 31/4 eth No. 31418 makes slow progress away from Leicester Station on 23 September 1983 as it passes London Road Junction signal box with the 0935 Norwich-Birmingham New Street cross country service.

Above - 4498 'Sir Nigel Gresley' approaches Knighton South Junction with the return 1L03 charter from Stratford-upon-Avon to Leicester on 7 June 1987. 'The Cromwell Pullman' was organised by Cromwell Tools, Wigston as a thank you to all is employees who helped organise their exhibition week at the factory and the NEC at Birmingham.

Above right - Passing Knighton South Junction on 4 May 1987 is Class 31/4 No. 31408 with the early morning 0614 Cambridge-Birmingham New Street service seen in brilliant lighting conditions.

Right - Leicester Shunter Class 08 No. 08474 propels a scrap train across the Midland Mainline at Knighton South Junction from Vic Berry's Scrapyard, Braunstone Gate on a trip working to Humberstone Road Sidings on 12 June 1986.

Left- IC125 HST set No.'s 43113 and 43100 in old blue livery with coaches in InterCity colours is seen using the slow line at Aylestone on 26 February 1986 in charge of the 12.50 Nottingham-London St Pancras service.

Below left - IC125 HST set 253025 (43050 and 43068) makes an unscheduled stop near Aylestone on 4 July 1983 as an obstacle had been placed on the line by vandals. The driver is seen climbing out of the Power Car of the 1100 Sheffield-London St Pancras service to remove the offending obstruction.

Right - Ex-works Class 31 No. 31120 in Railfreight livery waits at Hinckley Station on 26 June 1985 with the 2MO7 1728 Peterborough-Birmingham New Street service. The '31' was required at Saltley, Birmingham after re-paint at Doncaster BREL Works and was specially diagrammed for this duty.

Right - Class 20 locomotives No.'s 20013 and 20047 power away from Hinckley on 20 July 1985 with the 1E89 0740 SO Nuneaton TV - Skegness 'Jolly Fisherman' service. During the Hinckley holiday fortnight the 0816 SO Leicester service was extended to Nuneaton for three Saturdays for holidaymakers from this area to use thus saving them having to catch an earlier connecting service.

Far right - Class 47/4 conversion No. 47633 formerly No. 47083 'Orion' in large logo livery is seen on 20 January 1986 waiting alongside Croft signal box in the Quarry Sidings. The '47' will work the 7K03 ballast to Crewe Gresty Green later in the morning.

Right - Approaching Glen Parva Junction, South Wigston on 7 August 1987 is Class 58 No. 58004 in charge of the diverted 6M21 Didcot CEGB-Mantle Lane, Coalville MGR empties owing to derailment at Kingsbury on the Birmingham-Burton-on-Trent line.

Far right - An historic scene at Wigston South Junction on 3 June 1985. Class 45 No. 45135 '3rd Carabinier' heads towards Leicester with the 1D55 17.35 SX London St Pancras-Nottingham service.

Far left - Powering past the site of the former Wigston South Junction signal box is class 47/4 No. 47455 seen on 15 August 1987 with the 3C13 Derby-London St Pancras parcels.

Left - IC125 HST set no's 43051 and 43072 in new InterCity livery, with swallow motif, approaches Wigston North on 1 July 1987 with the 07.20 Sheffield-London St Pancras Master Cutler Pullman Service.

An interesting night scene at Leicester Station on 18 January 1988 finds InterCity 125 HST set No's 43051 and 43072 waiting on a wet evening with the 21.10 service to Sheffield. Alongside is Class 20 No. 20195 and Class 150/1, Sprinter No. 150112 stabled in between duties in the Post Office sidings.

Class 37/5 conversions No.'s 37502 'British Steel Teeside' in original Railfreight livery and 37501 'Teeside Steelmaster' in BSC Blue Livery trundle along the slow line at Cossington on 20 January 1988 with the 6M47 Lackenby BSC-Corby BSC 'Tubeliner'.

Trundling along the slow line again at Cossington on 29 October 1985 is Class 25 No. 25190 with a ballast train from Loughborough CCE Sidings bound for Nuneaton TV CCE Sidings on a beautiful sunny afternoon.

Single Class 150/2 No. 150205 and 150/1 No. 150144 units make an unusual sight at
Loughborough Station on 2 February 1989 with the 10.59 Nottingham-Coventry service.

Above - IC125 HST No.'s 43162 and 43058 passes Wigston North signal box on 16 June 1986 with the 12.50 Nottingham-St Pancras service. The line to the left is the branch to Nuneaton. Two weeks after this photograph was taken the signal box was rendered obsolete under Phase one of the Leicester Gap re-signalling scheme.

Left - Class 47 No. 47212 rumbles through Kegworth on 14 June 1988 hauling the 6E69 Langley-Humber Oil Refinery empty oil tankers.

Above - Class 56 No. 56093 runs off the branch line from Nuneaton at Wigston North Junction on 13 May 1987 with the 6D85 Three Spires Junction - Toton North Yard MGR empties.

Right - With the light fading very fast D200(40122) approaches Wigston North Junction from the South Junction on 4 May 1987 with the return Traintours Charter 'The Corby Cutler' from London St Pancras to Preston.

Far left - IC125 HST No.'s 43042 and 43195 rounds the curve between Wigston North and South Junctions on 13 May 1987 with the 0745 Nottingham-London St Pancras service.

Above - Consecutive Class 47/4 locomotives No.'s 47420 and 47419 pass Wigston South Junction signal box on Sunday 29 April 1984 with the 13.05 Nottingham-London St Pancras service. Due to operational reasons this service could be guaranteed to be Double Headed as an additional locomotive was required in London to work a late evening service back to Derby to ensure that the stock was available for the early morning weekday service.

Above right - Class 45/1 No. 45110 storms away from Wigston Magna on Sunday 10 May 1987 with the 1C11 1215 Sun Only Derby-London St Pancras service. The 'Peak' is seen carrying two commemorative headboards claiming that this was the last day farewell for Class 45 haulage on the Midland Mainline. However, it turned out it was 12 months later before finally the Class 45/1 was laid to rest from Midland Peak duties.

Left - Class 20 Bo-Bo's No.'s 20140 and 20078 take the spur line to Glen Parva Junction at Wigston South Junction triangle on 10 September 1987 hauling an engineers train from Wellingborough Old Yard to Nuneaton TV CCE Sidings. Included in the train is self-propelled heavy duty train jib crane No. DRP 78213, Plasser and Theurer RM74 ballast cleaner DR 76309.

Right - A working that invariably produced two locomotives was the 3C15 Derby-St Pancras newspaper empty vans. Unfortunately this popular evening working was lost in July 1988 when B.R. lost the newspaper contract. On 29 May 1987 Class 45/0 No. 45049 and Class 47/4 No. 47447 are seen at Kilby Bridge crossing near Newton Harcourt powering southwards towards Market Harborough.

Left - IC125 HST set No.'s 43098 and 43075 enters Market Harborough Station on 28 January 1989 in charge of the 1355 Leicester-London St Pancras service to collect a handful of passengers travelling south.

A royal visit to the Leicester-Nuneaton TV line on 19 April 1984 found Class 47/4 No. 47513 'Severn' in charge of the Royal Train seen between Hinckley and Nuneaton. The empty stock of the Royal Train was returning to Wolverton Works from Nottingham after taking the Queen and HRH Prince Philip to attend the Maundy Service at Southwell Minster.

Above left - For many years in the Eighties the Leicester-Birmingham line was well served by Class 31 stalwarts registering thousands of miles in charge of passenger services. On 16 August 1985 No. 31263 is seen at Jericho Crossing, Hinckley with the 2M07 17.28 Peterborough-Birmingham New Street service.

Left - In the late evening sunshine Class 31/4 eth locomotives No.'s 31418 and 31450 are seen alongside the signal box at Hinckley on 17 July 1986 with the 6A82 SX Toton West Yard-Willesden Brent Sidings ABS Railfreight heading towards Nuneaton TV where an electric locomotive will take over.

Above - Class 150 prototype unit No. 150002 approaches Hinckley station on 26 June 1985 with a special 2T05 1715 promotional service to Leicester in connection with a late night shopping evening to promote the Sprinter in this area before going into service from May 1986. In the following year this unit was modified at B.R. Derby and re-numbered to 154001.

45

Due to the closure of the NE/SW route between Birmingham and Derby on Sundays for engineering work during the summer of 1984 services were diverted via Leicester bringing IC125 HST sets to the Nuneaton-Leicester branch line. On 19 August 1985 HST 43185 and 43186 pass Hinckley Signal Box with 1E41 0800 Bristol Temple Meads-Newcastle service allowing Leicester passengers the luxury of travelling to Birmingham in comfort.

Class 40 No. 40155 is an unusual visitor seen passing through Hinckley Station on 11 January 1984 with a special 8L46 Toton Yard-Three Spires coal train. Throughout their working life 'Whistlers' made only spasmodic visits to the county much to the disappointment of local enthusiasts in charge of coal or stone trains. Four years later in January 1988 this locomotive was cut up at Crewe Works having been withdrawn at Carlisle three years earlier in January 1985.

Right - In Railfreight livery Class 47/3 No. 47378 is about to enter Hinckley Station on 9 October 1985 with the 7K03 Croft Quarry-Crewe Gresty Green departmental ballast. On arrival at Nuneaton TV the ballast train will be checked over thoroughly before being allowed to continue along the West Coast Mainline to Crewe.

Right - Not an everyday sight on the Nuneaton-Leicester line are Class 37 locomotives No.'s 37224 and 37159 seen down in Burbage Common Cutting near Hinckley on 5 August 1984 with a special Adex excursion 1Z38 Gloucester-Skegness.

Left - Class 31/4 locomotives No.'s 31410 and 31416 distinctive with silver grey roof power away from Hinckley on June 1985 with the 1020 SO Birming-ham New Street-Yarmouth summer service. From May 1988 Super Sprinters took charge of these services relegating the Class 31 loco's to more mundane duties of parcel or ballast workings.

Left - Class 47/4 No. 47457, later to be named 'Ben Line' is seen in blue large logo livery departing from Croft ECC Quarry Sidings on 17 January 1986 with the 7K03 Croft-Crewe Gresty Green departmental ballast. The ex-works Brush was on a running in turn from Crewe BREL Works after a recent overhaul.

Left - A scene of the past at Narborough Station on 26 August 1983 as a Class 120 three car DMU set No.'s 51573, 59285 and 51582 waits to depart with the 11.15 Birmingham New Street-Leicester service. Attached to the rear is a Class 105 two car set hitching a lift back to Leicester after working an earlier service from Cambridge. Narborough Station is noted for its flower bowls displayed on the platforms.

At Glen Parva Junction, South Wigston Class 25 No. 25265 is seen on 5 September 1986 with the early morning 6F10 FO Washwood Heath-Humberstone Road empty scrap wagons for use at Frank Berry's scrapyard, Leicester. Ironically nine months later this locomotive was to meet its fate in Leicester, when Vic Berry purchased condemned 25265 from Crewe and cut up the locomotive for scrap in his yard.

Above - Class 25/1 No. 25057 rounds the curve at South Wigston on 27 February 1986 passing the construction site of the new station due to open in ten weeks time. The '25' is conveying new Class 455/8 EMU's from York BREL Works back to Strawberry Hill after defective paintwork had been remedied.

Above right - It was a red letter day on 10 May 1986 when South Wigston Station was officially opened to the public by Leicester Lord Mayor at a cost of £135,000 paid for by the local authority. On the opening day a special half hourly service operated between Leicester and South Wigston and over 2,000 passengers took advantage of the new service. Class 150/1 Sprinters No.'s 150108 and 150144 are seen arriving at the station during the afternoon with a headboard depicting the famous occasion.

Right - A week after the opening of South Wigston Station a Charter train was operated by the 'Friends of South Wigston Station' to Llandudno. Class 47 No. 47351 is seen waiting at the staggered platform at the station with the 1L03 special from Leicester complete with a headboard on 17 May 1986.

Cromwell Tools, Wigston chartered 4472 'The Flying Scotsman' for the week 1-5 June 1987 to bring buyers from the British Industry meets its Suppliers exhibition stand at the NEC Birmingham to its factory in South Wigston. On the first day of the week, 4472, is seen having arrived at South Wigston with the charter of Pullman stock and will depart to Humberstone Road for stabling and taking on water until returning later in the afternoon to Birmingham.

Left - Approaching Rearsby Crossing on 11 January 1989 is Super Sprinter Class 156/4 No. 156410 with the 10.45 Norwich-Birmingham New Street Express Service on a sunny winters day.

Left - A few miles down the line from Rearsby Crossing is East Goscote Crossing and on 19 January 1989 Class 47 No. 47236 approaches with the Melton Sidings-Ardwick Pedigree Petfoods container train.

Left - Class 31/1 No. 31271 trundles towards Melton Mowbray from Kirby Bellars on 26 March 1986 with the daily 6E98 Mountsorrel Sidings-Peterborough West Yard departmental ballast. Semaphore signals are still in use in this area and it will be into the 1990's before colour lights replace them.

Above right - The old and the new at Melton Mowbray on 25 August 1988. New Class 156 Metropolitan-Cammell 23 metre Super Sprinter No. 156411 passes the old Melton station signal box in charge of the 11.41 Birmingham New Street-Cambridge service.

Right - A closer look at the new Super Sprinter as detailed above waits to depart from Melton Mowbray station, running to time.

Right - Two car Class 114 Derby works set T224 (54008 and 53008) departs from Oakham Station on 21 January 1989 with the 10.26 Birmingham New Street-Peterborough service seen about to pass Oakham Level Crossing signal box.

Left - Coalville became famous during the Eighties for holding Freight Open Days exhibiting BR freight and preserved diesels. However the biggest event was in 1987 when a locomotive naming ceremony took place in front of crowds of people, to name 47348 'St Christopher's Railway Home, after the local railway charitable home. The locomotive is seen before the un-veiling in pristine condition on 31 May 1987.

Left - Class 58 No. 58023 approaches Moira West Junction signal box on 24 March 1986 with a MGR coal train from Mantle Lane to Drakelow CEGB. On the left Class 58 No. 58025 waits at Rawdon Colliery with another MGR coal train for Willington CEGB. To the right are the remains of the Ashby-Nuneaton line closed in 1970 but remained open until 1984 to serve local collieries to Measham.

Right - One day in the year passenger trains run over the Leicester-Burton line to ferry passengers to Coalville attending the Freight Open Day. On 1 June 1986 the 2L21 special from Burton comprising of two Tyseley Class 116 DMU sets approaches Moira West Junction bound for the 1986 Open Day display. In the distance is Moira colliery and the famous section of track known as the 'Little Alps'.

No book on modern day Leicester would be complete without a look at Vic Berry's scrapyard Western Boulevard. On 4 September 1987 a total of 38 Class 25 and Class 27 locomotives are stacked in a mountain of three layers after having their bogies removed awaiting disposal in due course.